7-Day
Mind

By Rory James MacLaren-Jackson

Dear Vanessa,
Best wishes!
Rory M-J

ISBN: 978-1-326-01411-7

PublishNation, London
www.publishnation.co.uk

To all those who believe equality to be a right, not a privilege.

Table Of Contents

Foreword

Mindfulness truly seems to be the buzzword of the moment. Everyone seems to be talking about, or practising, Mindfulness. The reason for this seems quite clear, in that scientific research has proved its benefits, it is easy to practice and free from any doctrine.

In the past meditation was seen by many as esoteric, and only appealed to a certain type of individual. However, in recent times a leaner, cleaner, stripped-down form of meditation, called Mindfulness meditation has been promoted in the West. The scientific community has examined the benefits of practising Mindfulness with over 3,000 journal references. In 2013, a meta analysis of 209 such studies including over 12,000 participants found many benefits including "a large and clinically significant effect in treating anxiety and depression".

As a therapist I have known the benefits of meditation, in various forms, for many years. I have been fortunate enough to have studied with some of the greats in this field, including Zen Master Thich Nhat Hanh and His Holiness the Dalai Lama. I recall one teaching session with the Dalai Lama where the subject matter could best be described as 'hard going'. At one point I gazed around and saw that several of the students behind me had their heads down, eyes closed, and were breathing heavily. They would have said that they were 'deep in meditation'; however, to my trained Western eye, I could tell they were, in fact, asleep. It was at that time that I thought to myself: "If only there were a concise, easy-to-follow guide to meditation that got straight to the point."

So when Rory James MacLaren-Jackson told me he was writing this book I was excited by the prospect of a fast, effective guide to Mindfulness that could spread its benefits to everyone. A starting point, perhaps, on a voyage of self-discovery for today's overworked generation, who are too busy to go on a course or read a tome of a book the size of *War & Peace*. Rory M-J's practical, no-nonsense approach to therapy is reflected in **7-Day Mindfulness**, a guide which I am sure will bring a whole new insight into the lives of many.

It is estimated that 57% of books purchased are not read to completion and, given how long, dull and boring so many books are, I can understand why. However, **7-Day Mindfulness** gets to the heart of the matter, quickly and effectively, with morning exercises that are easy to follow. Commit both to read this book and practice the exercises within it, and watch the benefits unfold, enhancing your life in more ways than you can imagine.

Tim Williams
Harley Street
London

Preface

I have incorporated mindfulness into my therapeutic practice for a number of years and, alongside various other approaches and disciplines, it has both informed and supported my work as a Clinical Hypnotherapist.

Hypno-Mindfulness® developed out of this eclectic approach, with a practical focus on the techniques that prove most effective for each individual client. Essentially, it is an approach to mindfulness shaped by the theory, practice and experience of clinical hypnotherapy.

Over the years, I saw an increasing need in my own practice to create a mindfulness programme that could be followed by clients who would benefit from it, but who either doubted its value or, more often than not, doubted their own ability to effectively 'do' it.

I also received an increasing number of enquiries from people not wanting specifically to book a therapeutic session or even to learn mindfulness techniques in a formal setting, but rather looking for a good 'way in' to exploring mindfulness in their own time.

The response developed was *7-Day Mindfulness*: a short programme providing a simple yet powerful method to cultivate mindful awareness, incorporating the concepts, techniques and exercises that have proved of most benefit to my clients and also to me personally. There are also expanded versions of the programme, which I have developed since then for groups and delivery in organisational and corporate settings.

It is important to note that this is not a reference book. Together with the downloadable workbook, it is very much an instruction manual for individuals to use practically and has therefore been designed to be as straightforward and 'to-the-point' as possible. I have endeavoured to keep jargon to a minimum.

After just one week, like many people before, you may well feel a greater sense of yourself as a 'human being' rather than a 'human doing'. Feeling more in touch with one's self, many decide to carry on this positive journey further to explore what mindfulness can do for both mind and body.

Truth or Opinion

As with all of my contributions to the fields I work in, this book reflects the views and approaches that I have found to be of most benefit in my clinical experience.

Combined with evidence-based support for the effectiveness of mindfulness practice and for hypnotherapy, certain aspects of my clinical approach have become 'truth' to me. However, whether they are true for anyone else is for their personal consideration.

Free from speaking from any particular academic, political or ideological standpoint, I therefore humbly offer these views and approaches as *opinions* in the spirit of helping others to develop whatever physical and mental wellbeing they may seek.

nullius addictus iurare in verba magistri **– Horace**

Rory James MacLaren-Jackson
Dip. Hyp DNLP GQHP GHRreg
PgCert. Psychol. FRSA

Harley Street, London

www.rorymj.com

www.hypno-mindfulness.com

Rory M-J
Human Development

3

Introduction

"Are you a human being or a human doing?"

The modern world is a busy place… and getting busier.

As we rapidly move from one task to the next, constantly bombarded with information, our minds can become overwhelmed by the thoughts and feelings that naturally flow in response.

I see the consequences of this, in the form of the people seeking help at my clinical practice on a regular basis. The more disconnected we become from the moment, the more detached we are from our real 'self', we can begin to almost 'sleepwalk' into negative behaviours and conditions of the mind such as stress, anxiety and depression. Furthermore, in my specialist area of bad habit cessation, I often see the results of people trying to respond to, and self-medicate in dealing with, these resultant thoughts, feelings and conditions.

As a programme that I provide to many clients, the feedback I have received for **7-Day Mindfulness** has been overwhelmingly positive. Feeling more alive, calm, positive, centred and connected to the self are just some of the comments from them.

Whilst I often use hypnotherapy with my clients to make a 'breakthrough' in terms of positive change, for example stopping a bad habit or overcoming a fear or a phobia, combining this with regular self-hypnosis or mindfulness practice can often achieve the best results in the long-term. Hypnotherapy in this way could be seen as a kind of 'spring clean' of the mind, removing the clutter of negative thoughts and limiting beliefs. It follows that mindfulness is what I then teach my clients to *keep* the mind de-cluttered, and to help make the positive change sustainable in the future.

Hopefully after reading this book you will have a new, or at least another, perspective on how both everyday mindfulness and mindfulness meditation can benefit and enrich your life, with practical exercises and ideas to incorporate into your daily life and practice.

What Is Mindfulness?

Mindfulness is simply focusing one's attention on the moment and experiencing it with an awareness that is free from judgement and internal criticism.

Sounds simple enough, doesn't it? However, for some it can at times prove more difficult in practice.

One of the things such people often tell me is that they doubt their ability to "do" mindfulness and that they have "tried to meditate in the past, but always fail at it".

Trying to meditate in this instance is actually the problem itself – like trying to get to sleep, the very activity becomes the obstacle to the goal, of falling into sleep or, in the case of mindfulness meditation, just 'being'.

As we will explore, the beauty of mindfulness practice is precisely the spirit of non-judgement and acceptance that is cultivated. So, relax, knowing there is nothing to 'fail' at, just thoughts to ponder non-judgementally, and then gently *let... them... go*.

Lastly, though mindfulness has its roots in Buddhism and its great traditions, you can still benefit from it in a therapeutic context without engaging as part of a religious, spiritual or mystical experience. However, if you also wish to explore it as such then that path is always open to you.

The Benefits of Mindfulness

There is a large body of clinical studies supporting the therapeutic benefits of mindfulness practice for both the mind and body, with hundreds of new papers released annually in this popular area of research.

In recent years, Mindfulness-Based Cognitive Therapy (MBCT) has also been approved by the National Institute for Clinical Excellence (NICE) for use in the UK National Health Service (NHS).

Benefits of regular mindfulness practice can include:

- Healthily processing negative thoughts and feelings
- Reducing negative self-talk
- Reducing levels of stress and anxiety
- Better control of anger and angry outbursts
- Less sleep-onset insomnia
- Improving the relationship with pain and emotional responses to it
- Improving cognitive ability, including problem-solving and memory

- Increasing focus and concentration (increasing productivity)
- Improved communication and relationships with others

There is also increasing evidence to suggest that mindfulness practice does not just alter our perception of our physical body but also processes within it, for example strengthening the immune system by increasing the number of disease-fighting antibodies and improving the symptoms of conditions such as psoriasis and fibromyalgia. This is a very exciting area of research at present.

The Wandering Mind

"I was trying to daydream, but my mind kept wandering."
(Steven Wright)

With all this 'doing' it is easy to forget that we experience more inner peace and serenity when we are instead just 'being'.

When we are 'being', we are here, as in right here, as in right... NOW!

Simply 'being' is more difficult than it looks or sounds, because of the natural inclination of the human mind to wander. There is nothing wrong *per se* with the mind wandering – it relieves boredom, can in itself be relaxing and is often a source of creativity.

However, when our mind wanders it does have a propensity to time travel, either back into the past or projecting into the future – it is here where unhealthy or unproductive thought patterns can start.

We have probably all experienced being at a talk or lecture, knowing you have nothing to do other than listen, and your mind begins to wander to what you might be doing tomorrow, or next week, or even what you will be having for dinner later. That is your mind wandering from the 'here and now' to the future. Likewise, your mind might wander backwards in time and think about what a nice time you had last night or how well your breakfast meeting went.

It is also possible that you have been in such a situation and found your mind wandering back in time, maybe to that row you had with your partner in the morning, what you should not have said, perhaps guilt, anger or regret.

The Neuroscience of Mindfulness

It is outside the scope of this book to explore in detail the scientific theories on how mindfulness works in relation to the physical structures and processes in the human brain.

However, it is worthwhile to mention a theory that I believe helps to explain many of the benefits of mindfulness that studies have already proven, especially those related to the area of stress reduction.

In simple terms, when discussing the human brain, the **left hemisphere ('left brain')** is responsible for rational analysis and logical processing, whilst the **right hemisphere ('right brain')** is associated with abstract thought, creativity and emotional awareness.

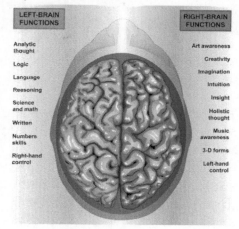

The problem is that we live in a very 'left-brain world', where our thinking is encouraged, even conditioned from an early age, to be rational, logical and fact-seeking. Our left-brain can become overloaded with information and often overwhelmed by the relentless pressure to make everything we experience fit into place or make sense. In turn, this pressure can lead to the engagement of the Sympathetic Nervous System (SNS) and the symptoms of stress indicative of the 'fight or flight' response – increased heart rate, increased blood pressure and slower digestion.

In addition, in trying to make everything we experience fit into place, the analytical left-brain spends a lot of time wandering up and down the 'timeline' of our existence, which explains the propensity of the mind toward the wandering that I alluded to. Conversely, the right brain is much more concerned with the 'here and now' and just 'being'.

When we practice mindfulness, we are effectively aiming to shift into right-brain dominant mode as we focus awareness away from left-brain analysis and logical thought and into right-brain feeling, intuition and sensation. Those moments where we struggle and start to 'think too much' during meditation or mindfulness practice can be seen as the left-brain 'fighting back' to maintain its dominance, for example thinking "I should be relaxing faster, I did better at mindfulness last night, why can't I do this better tonight? Oh no!" etc.

That is why we acknowledge those thoughts but then *let them go*, so we can return to the judgment-free (or analysis-free) awareness of the moment that typifies the right-brain dominant state of being. It follows that this state engages the Parasympathetic Nervous System (PNS) encouraging the 'rest and digest' response signified by lower blood pressure, lower heart rate and faster digestion. This goes a long way to explaining just one of the proven benefits of mindfulness practice – a reduction in stress levels.

As I mentioned there are many studies available if you wish to further explore the scientific basis for mindfulness practice, and I have included a list at the end of this book. These include scientific evidence of the benefits of mindfulness and meditation for physical health, mental health and general wellbeing.

The 7-Day Mindfulness Programme

This programme is designed to gently prompt and support the awakening of your mindful self by cultivating sensory awareness.

Following the programme you will be taking a week-long journey into exploring your self, your experience of life and the world around you.

Aside from the initial **'Awakening Awareness'** and the final **'Reflective Reflection'** day, the core middle days of the programme (Days 2-6) have distinct themes that the recommended daily practice and exercises are focused upon.

The themes of these days correspond to the 5 senses or the 5 representational systems as expressed in Neuro-Linguistic Programming (NLP). For those new to this term, NLP is an approach to communication, personal development and psychotherapy created by Richard Bandler and John Grinder in the USA during the 1970s.

Day	Representational System	Sense
1	Awakening Awareness	
2	Visual	Sight
3	Auditory	Sound
4	Gustatory	Taste
5	Kinaesthetic	Touch
6	Olfactory	Smell
7	Receptive Reflection	

In this book I shall be referring to each sense or system by the simpler descriptions found in the far right column.

NLP theorises that people tend to have a preferred representational style which influences how they interpret and interact with the external world, but also how they understand and map the internal world of their thoughts and emotions.

In this way I have applied the elements of NLP that inform my coaching and therapeutic style into the **7-Day Mindfulness** programme. The aim during the week is to gently explore, in a mindful way, ALL of the different types of sensory awareness.

Naturally, a preferred style will often emerge, but what matters more is the wonderful opportunity during this week to make *new* connections in your mind and body. It is a chance to explore mindfully those senses that you perhaps overlook, maybe even take for granted.

Daily Practice and Morning Meditation Exercise

Each day has an explanation of the specific theme being focused on and guidance on how you may wish to explore it during that day.

There will also be a single meditation exercise to be performed during the morning before your day starts. Reading the chapter and completing the exercise will take around 30 minutes.

In the evening before bed you can spend a few moments writing your reflections on the day in your personal workbook.

Preparation: The Week Ahead

There is, you may be pleased to hear, very little that you need to physically do to prepare for the *7-Day Mindfulness* programme.

All you will require for the programme is:

- You
- Awareness and adoption of the 'key attitudes' for fulfilling practice
- A printed 'hard copy' of the **'7-Day Mindfulness Workbook'** (downloadable at **http://www.7daymindfulness.com/workbook.pdf**)
- A pen / pencil
- A couple of everyday household items

Instead, it is about setting your mind up in such a way to get the most from the week, so in this chapter we will explore the key attitudes to adopt in order to ensure you fully engage with and enjoy the journey. It will also explain ways to maintain an open, positive mindset of receptivity and how to overcome any initial 'bumps in the road'.

The attitudes I recommend during the week are important so I want you to bring them to the forefront of your mind. This is done by physically writing down your thoughts and making a small promise to yourself after reading this chapter.

Pages 1-2 of the *7-Day Mindfulness Workbook* therefore act as a kind of informal contract with yourself

13

to reinforce your commitment and positive intention. You may find that the act of physically writing and signing it may also add a special resonance, as it often does.

7-Day Mindfulness: The Key Attitudes

For your mindfulness practice to be rewarding and fulfilling during the 7 days, there are certain attitudes, which I term **'Key Attitudes'**, that you should be both aware of adopting and maintaining. There are six key attitudes, plus one **'Ideal State'** which assists in bringing them all together.

These **Key Attitudes** form the foundation upon which successful mindfulness practice is built. As you may find, they also have considerable value in life far beyond your regular mindfulness practice.

However, it is important not to see these **Key Attitudes** as 'rules', as there should be no negative association with the pressure of success or failure. Instead, they are designed to cultivate awareness of the optimum path for fulfilling mindfulness practice. Just like with your meditation exercises, if you find you wander from the path, struggling to adopt a certain attitude, simply *notice* this and then gently guide yourself back on track.

When you are reviewing your day, the **Key Attitudes** also act as a review prompt as to which areas you may have found easy or difficult, allowing you to explore why this might be and how to develop in the future.

Key Attitude 1 – Patience

The Oxford Dictionary defines patience as *"the capacity to accept or tolerate delay, problems, or suffering without becoming annoyed or anxious"*.

When we are impatient, being annoyed or anxious are emotional *reactions* to certain events or stimuli. Often we will explain this emotional reaction as a direct effect caused by a certain event or experience. For example, a person might say, "of course I'm annoyed and angry, my train was delayed!" What they are doing is effectively stating that a delayed train causes annoyance and anger. But need it always and is it the case for everyone?

I am used to travelling around the country and the world with my work, so I always have a book to read (electronic these days) or device at hand for catching up with my emails. I would rather there was not a delay, but I do not feel angry or annoyed. In fact, especially when flying, I would rather they take their time and get all the important safety checks and preparation right rather than rushing!

By holding the above view or belief about delays, I do not *react* in the same way another person might. Instead I *respond* in such a way that does not cause me to get so easily emotionally disturbed. The Greek philosopher Epictetus stated how *'People are not disturbed by things, but by the views they take of them.'* Question the view you currently have, and find ways to re-shape it, perhaps viewing it from a different perspective.

For the **Key Attitude** of patience this means not striving or rushing, simply accepting that everything will unfold in due course. Just like how in nature things take their own time: the newborn chick breaks out of its shell when it is ready and not a moment before. In your mindfulness practice, simply acknowledge and notice impatient thoughts, then simply let them fade away.

Adopting this attitude during the week, and in life generally, you will experience the benefits of a healthy emotional *response* rather than an unhealthy, negative emotional *reaction*. This promotes emotional stability and a sense of centred, inner calm that increases resilience when facing life's challenges.

Key Attitude 2 – Trust

Trusting one's self can be challenging for those who are emotionally sensitive or who feel things deeply. Negatively focused, or even just too much, self-talk can lead an individual to 'second guess' and mistrust their thoughts and feelings.

The attitude to adopt, this week and beyond, is one of basic trust in yourself, your thoughts and your feelings. This trust acknowledges your fundamental authority, values your intuition and involves accepting responsibility for your own wellbeing. It also means understanding and accepting that you will not always be 'right' and that it is fine to make mistakes sometimes.

In your mindfulness practice, trust in *your* instincts, thoughts and feelings. No teacher, guru or even author (!) can have any more insight than you into *your* unique experience. Though your thoughts and feelings may not always reflect the facts of the situation, nor be what you necessarily expect to experience, they are what they are.

Simply trust in the ability of your inner wisdom to guide you, through your practice and through each day.

Key Attitude 3 – Non-Judgement

This is one of the most important attitudes to cultivate and maintain during mindfulness practice and for more mindful living.

The critical mind, which can be termed the "inner critic", passes judgement almost continuously both on the world we interact with but also on our own internal thoughts and feelings. In fact the inner critic excels at passing judgement – on others, the world at large and especially on us ourselves. It follows that it is here that the cycle of negative and potentially damaging self-talk can often begin.

The ability to judge and analyse critically is of course invaluable in navigating our world. However, this rapid, automatic process can be less helpful for our thoughts and feelings. Like everything else we experience, we rush to automatically label and value them as good/bad, helpful/unhelpful, positive/negative, happy/sad, inspiring/de-motivating, etc.

This is most noticeable for those who have tried (in their view unsuccessfully) to meditate previously. It is often the inner critic that causes frustration when meditating of "not being able to do it" – that little voice saying "this feels silly" or "I've had a bad day, I can't relax", etc.

Practising non-judgement during mindfulness practice means acknowledging but then silencing that inner critic. In essence, there is no success or failure when practising mindfulness. When you experience a thought or feeling, you can still label it. You may think "oh, that's an angry thought" or "that's a sad thought", but then remind yourself that it is only a thought, that there may be many other ways to look at it and then let it go, free from value, free from judgement.

In everyday life, this is a key attitude that many find incredibly beneficial, as practising non-judgement effectively means cultivating an awareness of your mind's propensity to judge automatically and taking steps to regain control and reserve this judgement.

For example, employing the mindful attitude of non-judgement when angered by someone involves not automatically following an angry thought and reacting, but rather taking a moment to observe those thoughts and feelings you are experiencing. In this case, you could label the thought as an angry one, but remove any judgement or value, perhaps asking yourself whether there is another way to see the situation. All the time knowing that a thought is simply a thought and not reality.

In this way non-judgement as a key attitude of mindfulness is about better understanding your judgements and your self. Which of them do you think through in a balanced way and which are snap, automatic judgements? Adopting a non-judgemental attitude in your life and mindfulness practice will enable you to firstly pause and then get perspective on any thoughts or feelings that you are experiencing.

Key Attitude 4 – Acceptance

The attitude of acceptance follows on naturally from the attitude of non-judgement – that we can be aware of our experiences without engaging with them emotionally.

Accepting our feelings in life can be difficult at times because of certain patterns that the human mind has a habit of falling into. For example, when we have an experience that upsets us, we might feel bad. However, feeling bad can then become a downward spiral when we start to feel bad about feeling bad, and so on.

Cultivating an attitude of acceptance is about more than just "putting up" with the experiences that bother us. I am sure we have all had that unhelpful advice from people before! Instead, it is about acknowledging the feeling, taking a step back and then exploring it in a calmer, more detached way.

Whether during everyday life or dedicated mindfulness practice, a route to acceptance is to identify the nature of the feeling you are experiencing. I refer to this with my clients as 'exploring' the feeling. This can be done by closing your eyes, taking a deep breath and then considering the feeling for a moment: where is it located in your body, does it have size, a shape, a colour, a rhythm or a texture? As you explore, you will find that you create a distance between what you are experiencing and the emotional response it creates. In this way feelings can become smaller, more manageable and, in a mindful sense, more acceptable.

Key Attitude 5 – Non-Attachment

Just as we can be aware of our experiences non-judgementally, without engaging with them emotionally, we can also cultivate an attitude of non-attachment to these experiences. This means neither holding on to them nor pushing them away.

As with the other key attitudes, the importance of non-attachment is mirrored in everyday life as it is during dedicated mindfulness practice. When a thought, feeling or experience is pleasurable for us we are inclined to cling to it, to sustain and prolong it. Conversely, when this creates an unpleasant or painful association, we often try and actively reject or deny it.

As you have already seen with the key attitude of non-judgement, by removing the need to attribute a value of positive or negative, we can just observe the experience, without amplifying any positive association or diminishing a negative one.

In this sense, cultivating an attitude of non-attachment is about 'letting go' or disengaging from the experience, thought or feeling. Instead just observing each moment, one after the other, free from judgement.

If during your mindfulness practice you find yourself clinging to a thought, feeling or sensation, firstly become aware you are doing so, remark how interesting an idea that is, then having observed it, just let it go. Almost like loosening your grip on the string of a helium balloon, the string slips through your fingers and the balloon, like that thought or feeling, just drifts away as you let go.

It is this feeling of 'letting go' that people sometimes say they have had difficulty with during previous attempts to meditate, even going as far as to describe how they "just can't let go". In fact, we all have the built-in ability to let go, the only obstacle is *trying* too hard so that the activity itself becomes a barrier.

Every night we fall asleep and it is always easiest when we do not try, but simply when we just relax and 'let go'. Letting go in a mindful sense is about falling not into sleep, but falling into the present or the moment, with an attitude of non-attachment to any thoughts, feelings or sensations that arise.

Key Attitude 6 – 'New Born' Curiosity

This is one of the most rewarding and enjoyable of the **Key Attitudes** to cultivate during the next seven days, both in your everyday life and dedicated mindfulness practice.

Firstly, the attitude I recommend adopting is one of child-like curiosity, imagining what it would be like if you were experiencing a sensation or experience *for the very first time*. It can be quite a profound experience to re-connect with yourself and the world with a sense of wonder and excitement.

Likewise, often when people have an experience that brings the idea of their own mortality into their consciousness, they describe how it literally brings their senses into focus. Perhaps contemplation that we will not always be here to experience all the wonders of life encourages us to savour the time and experiences we have left.

Secondly, this curiosity should be gently investigative and questioning of your experiences, sensations, thoughts and feelings; especially during your practice. A good starting point is guiding your thoughts with the questioning phrases "I wonder..." and "How interesting..." to delve into these experiences and explore them further. This can further blossom into a curious "Ha!" or "Well, how about that?"

Curiosity is valuable for cultivating mindful awareness because it connects us directly to the present by focusing our attention on the moment. If you have ever seen a child experience something for the first time you will know what intense curiosity looks like – usually a complete fascination with exploring this new thing in their world. At that moment there is absolutely no thought of the past or the future, just trying to explore and absorb everything about it.

You may not only have seen that in children but, of course, at one point you were that child. We all start life with a great natural capacity for mindfulness and open-heartedness, but we lose touch with the ability to connect to the moment as the years pass. Building up the baggage of the past and worries about the future, these become constant distractions from the phenomena happening right in front of us in the here and now.

Throughout your day, look for opportunities to gently and honestly explore fresh perspectives on familiar thoughts, feelings, people, places and situations. *Experience them*, as much as you can, as if you had never encountered them before, and take this 'new born' curiosity into your daily practice too.

Ideal State – 'Embracing The Moment'

Whilst there are **6 Key Attitudes** that form the foundation for a successful 7 days of mindfulness, there is one overarching **Ideal State** and that is one of **'embracing the moment'**.

You could say that adopting the **6 Key Attitudes** leads to this state, but it is also important to keep it in your mind as a reminder, since it is in itself very much the essence of mindfulness.

Just asking your self the question "Am I embracing the moment?" or "Am I here, right now?" can be the prompt required to bring yourself back to the present moment.

The word embracing is carefully chosen too, because this week is not just about opening your mind, but also opening your heart to the potential of being more mindfully aware.

So, embrace the moment with a warm, generous spirit of playful curiosity, free from judgement or expectation.

Setting Your Radar

As each day involves cultivating a mindful awareness around a given theme, a good way of expressing this is setting your 'radar' to the specific type of sensory awareness being explored each day.

There will also be an affirmation or mantra provided each day to help focus your mind on the theme. You might want to add a sticky note of this on your desk or in front of your diary each day.

In this way you can keep the sensory theme of the day in the forefront of your mind as you experience the world around you in a more mindful way.

Morning Meditation

You will need to make a half hour time slot available first thing in the morning for the prescribed mindfulness exercise of each day.

I recommend drinking a cool glass of water (perhaps with a slice of lemon) before starting, which creates a lovely fresh, cleansed feeling.

Ideally you should sit on a straight-backed chair, like a dining room chair, feet flat on the ground, hands resting on knees or lap.

For most of the exercises, there will be no specific movements to perform, so try and keep as still as possible overall. But where you do occasionally move, try and make those movements as small, slow and smooth as possible, in order to help you remain calm and focused.

Developing A Skill Takes Time

Don't forget that whilst mindfulness may be a state of awareness, practising it is also a *skill*.

In this way it is similar to playing the harmonica or mouth organ. Even the most non-musical person can get a tune out of the instrument with a small amount of practice; but mastery, performing to a high level almost every time, takes *practice*. Just like with other skills, some days it will be easy, other days it will be difficult; some days it will be enjoyable, some days it will feel like a chore.

As with anything, the more you practice, the more skilled you become and the more scientifically-proven rewards of mindfulness you will benefit from.

Remember – Download your *7-Day Mindfulness Workbook* here:

http://www.7daymindfulness.com/workbook.pdf

7-Day
Mindfulness

Day 1

Awakening Awareness

"Becoming mindful of your breathing and breath is a fantastic place to start and to awaken your awareness."

The average person breathes around 28,000 times a day – that makes over 10 million breaths a year.

You are breathing all the time, even when sleeping, yet how often do you think about this amazing life-sustaining process? For most people the answer is 'not very often'.

Unless attention is drawn to our breathing, either by someone suggesting to us to think about it or by noticing something wrong (such as being short of breath or experiencing a pain when breathing), then it simply happens automatically.

There is, of course, nothing wrong with this; this is how it is designed to happen. The conscious mind has enough to deal with without having to constantly remember to breathe in and out.

However, as you will often discover with mindfulness during this week, just because we can do something 'on autopilot' does not mean we always should. In fact, in always doing so, we are often denying ourselves the physical and mental benefits of being more mindfully aware of the experience.

This is why becoming mindful of your breathing and breath is a fantastic place to start and to awaken your awareness. You will not be doing anything that you have not already done almost every minute of your life since the moment you were born.

Morning Meditation – 'Mindfulness of Breath'

Sitting or lying comfortably, eyes closed or open, just gently focus your attention on your breathing.

Just notice each breath as it happens. You might notice how the air feels as it flows through your nostrils travelling into your lungs or you may notice how your chest rises and falls and your abdomen expands and contracts. Simply observe each breath as it happens, whether you focus on the rise and fall of your chest or abdomen, or on the sensation of your breath at the nostrils.

Just notice, observe, what your breathing feels like. Do not make any inferences, judgments or conclusions, just observe.

As you engage in this exercise you may find that your mind wanders, caught by thoughts or by noises in the room, or bodily sensations. Or you might wander to thoughts of the past or the future, maybe even what you did yesterday or things you have to do later, after your practice.

When you notice your mind wandering in any of these ways, know that this is okay; simply notice the distraction but gently bring your attention back to the breath. No judgment, no comment, just gently guiding your awareness back to your breath.

It is almost like your awareness is an inflatable beach ball, gently riding the waves of your breaths, however they ebb and flow.

And if you can, for the very last part of your practice, maybe just allow yourself to let go of all remaining awareness. All sounds, thoughts, feelings, even your breath, let it all sink down into one deep, peaceful state of being. Feel complete, whole, experiencing that sense of 'oneness' of self.

Wow, You Did It!!

Guess what? You have just practiced mindfulness and because there is no judgement, no success or failure, you have taken the first step on a truly enriching and rewarding journey.

Remember – Now take a moment to record your reflections on this morning's exercise in your workbook. Do not think too much about what to write, just write down your thoughts and feelings as they flow following the session.

Daily Practice

For today, simply find the time to practice this mindfulness meditation **three times** if you can.

Practice at different times, maybe different locations. Maybe you will find an opportunity to practice in the morning, in a break at work or during the day and again in the evening. You may notice it is different each time, but guide your awareness away from any judgements or commentary DURING your practice.

At the end of the day, you can take the time to peacefully reflect on this first 'awakening' day of mindfulness and note down your reflections on the experience in your workbook.

7-Day
Mindfulness

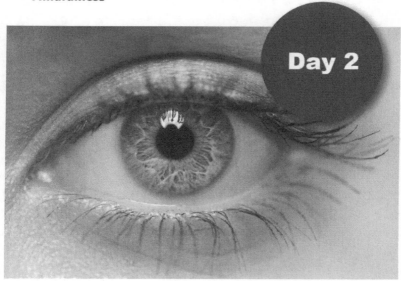

Day 2

Mindfulness of Sight

"I am seeing with fresh eyes"

Sight is one of the senses we are most dependent on and relate to our experience of the world through. However, what we 'see' and what we perceive visually are very different and it is a much more complex process (or set of processes) than we often realise.

Our eyes are vital for this process, with a lens in each eyeball helping to focus images onto the retina at the back of the eye. The retina is covered with special light sensitive cells – 'cones' which allow us to see colour and 'rods', which allow us to see light/dark, shape and movement. The information received by these cells is sent via the optic nerve to the brain.

The most dramatic example of the difference between seeing and visual perception is the fact that the images sent from the eyes to the brain are actually upside down. It is our brain that turns them the right way up and also combines the images from both eyes to create a three-dimensional image, creating the perception of depth.

Cognitive psychology often explores in great depth how our visual perception is more than just *what* we see, but effectively *how* we see it. Our experience of visual awareness is often influenced by the brain 'filling in gaps' or making inferences or assumptions from the information received. For example, if you see someone with their back to you facing a window, you might say that you SEE them looking out of the window.

But what do you actually SEE?

Without seeing the person's eyes, all you have really seen is the person FACING the window. You have therefore inferred, even imagined, that their eyes are open, when in fact it is just as likely they are closed.

You SAW a person facing a window, but you PERCEIVED a person looking out of a window.

Sight – There Is A Lot To Take In!

The example above is just one illustration of how we have evolved, quite usefully, to have an intuition based on experience and the patterns we observe in terms of what we are seeing.

In general, more often than not, a person facing a window is looking out of it, so it is useful to make that instant visual judgement. Bombarded with new visual information all day long, it is helpful to keep our minds free to process it by 'taking for granted' things that we are used to seeing, However, as you can see with the inferential error explored above, there is a potential to miss out on things that we could benefit from seeing.

Today, we are going to explore the sense of sight mindfully, an opportunity to literally look at yourself and the world around you in a new way. People often find this a particularly rewarding and profound experience of the 7 days.

Morning Meditation

Sitting comfortably, either outside or where you have access to a view outside, take a moment to focus on an object or aspect of the natural world. An example could be a plant, a tree, a flower, an insect or animal or even just the clouds in the sky.

As you look at what you have chosen, do not do anything other than notice and observe it, almost like you are seeing it for the very first time. Explore visually every aspect and detail of this natural thing: its colour, shape, perceived texture, sense of weight, any movement but also its purpose, its possibilities, its place in the world in this very moment.

Engage in a playful spirit of curiosity, maybe feeling that child-like sense of wonder, and letting yourself become consumed by the presence and infinite possibilities of this chosen object of your attention.

As you notice, calmly observing, you may feel a growing connection so simply enjoy the feeling of just looking, observing and being.

Remember – Now take a moment to record your reflections on this morning's exercise in your workbook. Do not think too much about what to write, just write down your thoughts and feelings as they flow following the session.

Daily Practice

Daily Mantra: *"I am seeing with fresh eyes"*

Keep the above thought in your mind, repeating when you can, as a reminder to engage your sense of sight in a more mindful way as you go about your day.

Adopting the key attitudes, especially 'new born' curiosity, you will find many ways to mindfully engage your sense of sight.

Here are just a few ideas:

- Look up as you go about your daily routine – what interesting architecture or aspects of nature might you have neglected simply because they are above your natural eye level?

- During the day, notice the clouds, their shape, their movement – do they remind you of anything? At night, you might notice the stars or the twinkle of artificial lights.

- Notice the colours, and perhaps the makes, of the cars you see passing by in traffic.

- Are people you pass smiling? Preoccupied? Showing particular emotions? Sometimes if you are smiling, they might then smile too, be aware of changes.

- When watching TV, take a moment to not watch the star actors but watch the lesser actors or the extras, even the furniture or background objects in the scene.

- When watching a sports match, take a break from watching the ball and instead watch what the other players are doing.

7-Day
Mindfulness

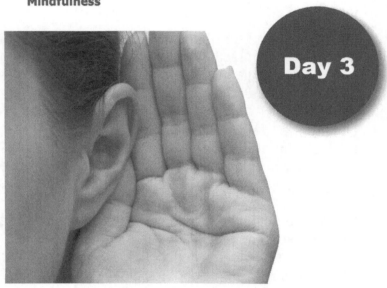

Mindfulness of Sound

"I listen to the sounds around me"

Our sense of sound is engaged constantly throughout our waking day, allowing us to communicate via language and providing important information about our environment, such as the distance and direction of sounds we hear.

Vibrations captured by the 'cup' of the outer ear travel to the tympanic membrane and then onto the inner ear (or 'cochlea'), which translates them into sound messages sent to the brain via the auditory nerve.

As with sight, there is a difference between the information we receive and how we perceive it. On a basic level, there is a difference between hearing and listening – the former being more passive and the latter a more active process.

For example, you might hear the 'noise' of a radio in the background, but not be listening to exactly what song or discussion it consists of. If you are listening to the song, you may be listening to the music without catching the lyrics. Once again, our brain filters out and allows our attention to be selective.

The ability to tune in to what we want to listen to and tune out those things that we do not is highly valuable. For example, there may be lots of people talking in a busy room, but you are able to focus on, listen to and comprehend the person you are talking to (providing the background sounds are not too loud or too distracting).

However, it also often means that we are missing out on exploring a large part of the 'soundscape' of our daily lives. This is especially true of the sounds we hear regularly or those things we often listen to. Again, we start to take them for granted and form a habit of listening in the same way each time we hear something familiar.

This is especially true of music where a particular genre, artist or song can take us back to a fond memory of the past or alter our emotions. This is of course enjoyable in itself, but overlooks the potential to practice mindful awareness in the present when listening to music.

Morning Meditation

For this exercise you will need a piece of music to listen to: ideally one that you have not heard before, yet perhaps interests or intrigues you somehow.

There may be such a piece already in your collection or you could browse online for a suitable track. Alternatively, you might choose to scan radio stations for something suitable.

Many people enjoy this exercise using headphones and either sitting or lying comfortably with their eyes closed, in order to fully focus on the sounds being heard.

As you listen to the song, focus all of your attention on the different sounds you can hear, layers of complexity and intricacy. If your mind wanders to thoughts about the artist, genre or different instruments you hear, gently guide your awareness back to what is being played or sung.

As a test, it is possible to focus your hearing on certain types of sound within the composition: "now I'm listening to the lead violin", "now I'm listening to the accompanying woodwinds…" Or with modern music, you can listen to the different layers or rhythms placed on top of each other (the bass, the lead vocalist, the backing track, etc). When you do this, you are in control of what your brain filters, rather than it happening automatically. You are truly listening.

As your awareness becomes focused on the sound of the music you can let it resonate with your being.

Remember – Now take a moment to record your reflections on this morning's exercise in your workbook. Do not think too much about what to write, just write down your thoughts and feelings as they flow following the session.

Daily Practice

Daily Mantra: *"I listen to the sounds around me."*

Today's practice is very much about setting your 'sonar radar' to hear and then listen mindfully to both new sounds and those more familiar ones you may have been filtering out. Some ideas to help you include:

- Listen for ambient sounds you might not usually catch – air conditioning/heating, electronic devices droning, clock ticking?

- Background music around you.

- People talking around you – at work, on public transport, restaurants etc.

- Birds / nature?

- Your own voice – how you sound normally, and how you may sound slightly different in certain situations (higher, lower, faster, slower etc.)

- Your own breathing, laughs, coughs, sniffles, sighs, yawns etc.

- The rustling of your clothes or the noise of your shoes when you walk/move.

- Noises made by common things you use all the time – computer, toothbrush, drinking glass / mug, cooking implements, turning the pages of a book…

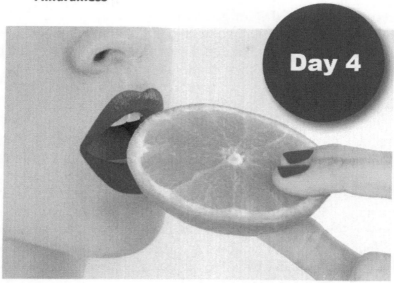

Mindfulness of Taste

"I taste and savour every mouthful"

Our sense of taste comes from combined information that we receive both from the taste buds (or papillae) on the surface of our tongue and from another sense, that of smell (which you will explore on its own during Day 6).

In terms of taste, the tongue can only detect four distinct flavours – sweet, sour, salty and bitter. However, these four flavours can be present and interact in an almost infinite number of taste combinations. The tongue also allows us to explore and understand both the texture and temperature of the things that we put in our mouth.

Tasting is naturally most associated with eating and drinking, and it is here that we have all had experiences of different levels of mindfulness in relation to these activities. For example, anyone who has an issue with snacking too much (often on unhealthy foods) will know that it is easy to eat a packet of crisps or a chocolate bar without paying much attention. One minute the snack is in your hand, next minute, all gone! I have had weight loss clients who say they then feel almost cheated because they did not get to enjoy the first crisps or chocolate bar, so feel justified in having another. A lot of my work with helping people lose and control their weight involves this shift from unconscious or autopilot eating to mindful eating.

When one thinks of very mindful eating and drinking, good examples are wine tasting, tea tasting, or indeed any form of food or drink connoisseurship. A connoisseur is essentially someone practising a highly mindful awareness of the experience they are engaging in. In the case of wine or tea tasting, this mindfulness is evident in the multi-sensory appreciation of the drink: noticing its colour, its texture, sniffing its aroma, savouring its taste slowly in different parts of the mouth. The connoisseur is really there in the moment when tasting the drink.

When we gulp down our food or drinks in haste, aside from the digestive ill effects that can arise, we are missing out on the benefits of experiencing mindfulness of taste. By exploring this type of mindfulness many experience new enjoyment and appreciation of what they eat and drink plus find it easier to control their diet, separating eating from emotions.

Morning Meditation

For this exercise you will need a couple of grapes, berries, raisins or, for those chocoholics amongst us, a couple of squares of chocolate.

Sitting comfortably, place two of your selected snacks in front of you, ideally on a white plate or napkin. Take a deep breath and just let your vision focus on, using grapes in this example, one of the two grapes.

What does it look like? Notice its size, texture, its surface and colour. Maybe there are different colours. Perhaps it looks softer in some parts than others. Ponder for a moment of its story, where it came from, where in the world it may have grown on a vine, and its journey to be here now in front of you. Now direct your attention to the other grape, notice it again in the same way, but compare too – is it smaller or larger, shaped differently, does it look juicier?

Now it is time to make a choice, select one of the grapes and slowly pick it up with your thumb and forefinger. How does it feel, is the texture different to the touch than it appeared by sight? If you squeeze very gently can you get a sense of the moisture of the fruit inside? You can also see it much closer now, are there other colours and surface shades that you can see under closer examination?

You might already have a sense of anticipation at this point, so now it is time to taste! Close your eyes and gently place the grape in your mouth. Don't bite yet, just let it roll around your mouth. Perhaps there is already a taste hinted at. Explore its shape and texture with your tongue.

Do this for a few moments and then your reward comes: bite into the grape! Feel that explosive release of the grape juice, the sweet flavour, but also the different textures that your tongue and mouth can now explore – the soft, succulent moistness of the fruit. Notice how the intensity of the flavour changes as you chew, how different flavours and levels of sweetness may ebb and flow. Then, as you swallow, what flavour is left, does it stay or fade and at what rate?

When ready open your eyes, reflect on mindfully tasting that grape and repeat the process again with the second one.

If you have time you can repeat this exercise again in the evening. If you like chocolate then it can be a wonderful way to sensually experience its unique taste and the sensations it brings.

Remember – Now take a moment to record your reflections on this morning's exercise in your workbook. Do not think too much about what to write, just write down your thoughts and feelings as they flow following the session.

Daily Practice

Daily Mantra: *"I taste and savour every mouthful"*

As you eat and drink throughout the day, make a conscious effort to be more mindful, both when having snacks or during your main meals.

Remove anything else that might usually distract you as you eat and drink – do not watch TV, read, etc; rather focus your attention on the food in front of you and its taste. If you are having lunch with others you can still engage in conversation, but not as you are eating. Once you have spoken for a moment then gently focus your attention back to the experience of the food and your sense of taste.

Useful tips during the day that others have found of benefit:

- Slow down when eating, taking your time to enjoy each mouthful.

- When tasting your food try and identify the flavours, for example the individual ingredients in a sauce.

- Sip drinks slowly: notice the difference between the initial taste and any aftertastes, do they quench your thirst or stimulate it?

- Snacks, mints, nuts, chocolate, fruit – when was the last time you mindfully tasted them? – from looking at the packet to placing in your mouth. Close your eyes and try to taste them as if it is the first time.

- Toothpaste, mouthwash – often we look after our teeth as part of our autopilot routine but there is taste to explore here too.

- Notice the various tastes in different parts of your mouth – let your tongue explore your teeth, gums, inside of cheeks and lips.

Day 5

Mindfulness of Touch

"I connect with my touch"

The sense of touch is the result of nerves spread throughout the body and nerve endings in the skin sending information to the brain.

We mostly differentiate between the varying sensations of hot, cold, contact and pain. The hair on our skin, covering large parts of our body, can also provide advance warning of our sense of touch being about to be activated.

Our hands and fingertips have a high concentration of nerve endings and are how we most commonly interact consciously with the world through the sense of touch.

Just as we might find ourselves hearing but not mindfully listening to the sounds around us, we can also take our physical contact with the world around us for granted, neglecting the full experience of our sense of touch. By contrast, with practice, your awareness of touch can be boosted to a level of great sensitivity, as can be seen in doctors, pianists, or American football wide receivers (those whose job it is to catch the ball), all of whom can be colloquially described as 'having good hands'.

Morning Meditation

Select a small everyday object from your home for this exercise, for example an ornament, a watch, piece of jewellery, item of clothing or even something from the natural world like a leaf. If possible try and choose an item that does not have a strong emotional association to it, either positive or negative.

Placing the object on a surface in front of you, take a deep breath and gently guide your attention to the object. Firstly look at it, can you imagine what it feels like, notice its shape, texture and surface. Can you already sense its weight and how it might feel in your hands?

Then gently pick up the object, maybe closing your eyes to further heighten and isolate your sense of touch. What does it feel like, in whole or in part? Is it smooth or uneven, hard or soft, flexible or rigid? Does it feel heavy or light? When you rest it in one hand, can you balance it? Is it cool or warm to the touch, or perhaps does it warm up as it is in your hands?

Mindfully explore the object for around 10 minutes, with the attitude of 'new born' curiosity as if it were the very first time you have felt it. If you have closed your eyes for most of the exercise, perhaps gently open your eyes at times, to look again as you feel it. If this distracts, simply close your eyes again and return to the feeling of the object in your hands, gently guiding your awareness back to it.

Remember – Now take a moment to record your reflections on this morning's exercise in your workbook. Do not think too much about what to write, just write down your thoughts and feelings as they flow following the session.

Daily Practice

Daily Mantra: *"I connect with my touch"*

Since so much of our everyday routine involves touch, the way in which we interact with our world kinaesthetically provides a fantastic opportunity during the day to achieve a state of mindful awareness.

- Notice and explore with 'new born' curiosity those common items you pick up and use – at home, at work, or elsewhere.

- When using your phone or computer – typing, pressing buttons, clicking the mouse – notice the sensations in your hands and fingers.

- Notice the feeling of your clothes on your skin as you move or sit still.

- Observe the feeling of touch when interacting with other people, for example when shaking hands, the strength of their grip, etc.

- Take a moment to look at your hands, your fingers. Hold them up, feel how sensitive they are even to the air around them when you become mindful of them. Wave a hand back and forth a few times very fast whilst keeping the wrist rigid – can you feel the air resistance against your skin as you do so?

- When going to the bathroom at night, try to avoid switching on the lights and use your sense of touch to assist your night-vision – guide yourself by gliding a hand along the walls as you walk, feel the door handle as you gently push it open, etc. *(Note: please be careful not to hurt yourself in the dark!)*

Mindfulness of Smell

"I breathe in the scent of my experience"

Our sense of smell is active and processing information all the time, and yet often it is a sense we are not mindful of unless we are consciously 'smelling' something or we notice something smelling particularly good or bad.

It is the fumes of various substances that make up the different smells we experience. Molecules of these react with small receptors found in the mucous membrane of the nose, which are connected to the olfactory nerve.

As with taste, there are a number of different, distinct types of smell that we can register: camphor, musk, flower, mint, ether, acrid and putrid. Likewise, as with taste, these can combine to create uniquely layered complex scent combinations.

When we mindfully engage our sense of smell we are exploring one of our most neglected senses and one that adds an excellent dimension to mindfulness practice.

Morning Meditation

For this exercise you should use something that has a strong scent such as coffee beans, or a strong-scented perfume, flower or plant.

Sit comfortably and close enough to the item to sense its scent. Then close your eyes and take a deep breath through your nostrils. What exactly do you smell, can you identify the component smells, is the scent layered? Is it stronger in places, does it become harder to detect with time as you become accustomed to it, does it change as you get used to it?

Continue this sensory exploration for around 10 minutes.

> **Remember** – Now take a moment to record your reflections on this morning's exercise in your workbook. Do not think too much about what to write, just write down your thoughts and feelings as they flow following the session.

Daily Practice

Daily Mantra: *"I breathe in the scent of my experience"*

During the day remind yourself to breathe through your nostrils and seek out those smells around you, allowing you to explore them mindfully.

- Smells on the train/tube/bus – someone else's perfume or the food someone is eating

- Your car – 'new car' smell, old pleasant or unpleasant smells?

- The meals you eat, or smells in the places where you obtain food (kitchen, sandwich shop, restaurant, work canteen, supermarket)

- Drinks – coffee, tea, fizzy drink, even water (the absence of smell)

- Snacks – in particular, smell fruit before and after peeling

- Various ambient smells – air freshener? Bad smells like pollution? Your soap, shampoo, shower gel? Disinfectant and cleaning products? Sweat at the gym?

- If you live in proximity to them, any natural smells – trees, rain, soil, river, pets…

Day 7

Receptive Reflection

"Relaxed mind, receptive mind"

This final day of the **7-Day Mindfulness** programme provides the opportunity to combine and experience, in a more holistic way, the different types of sensory awareness that have been awakened during the week.

It is a day of receptivity, opening all sensory channels, rather than just focusing on any individual sense or theme. It is also a day to review and reflect on the experience and benefits of having explored mindfulness in both an everyday sense and through your dedicated meditation practice.

The **'Complete Sensory Awareness'** meditation for today, like the 'Mindfulness of Breath' exercise from Day 1, is one that is recommended for regular use and is a great way to connect to the moment at any point, calming the mind and body.

The rewards and even enjoyment from this particular mindfulness meditation are enhanced by virtue of the preceding six days of cultivating mindful sensory awareness. Like old friends you may not have had much contact with for a while, having 'caught up' with all of your senses, this re-engagement is not only satisfying in its own right but has significant benefits for future practice.

Morning Meditation

Start by sitting on a straight-backed chair, feet flat on the ground and hands resting on your knees or lap. To begin with, let your eyes close down.

Now take some relaxing breaths – breathing deeply in and fully exhaling out. As with Day 1, just calmly observe your breaths. If your mind wanders anywhere else, gently guide your awareness back to your breathing.

After a couple of minutes, with your breathing at a calm steady level, it is time to begin a gentle tour of your senses, engaging them one by one. At this point some people like to open their eyes, or others wait until later in the meditation when it is required – it is entirely up to you.

For each sensory step allow around 2-3 minutes.

Sound: Firstly, guide your awareness to the sounds around you, notice them, but as always keep this observation free from any judgement. Perhaps guide your awareness to one sound, exploring that, before moving on to another, your awareness rather like a bee gently hovering from one flower to the next. Finally, observe the whole 'soundscape' – as if listening to a symphony of noises, buzzes, hums, even the sound of your own body. Notice how they combine and take a few moments to let all of these sounds wash over you.

Smell: Next, gently guide your awareness onto what you can smell around you. Take a few deep breaths in through your nose, this time mindful not of the flow of air but rather the scents in your environment. Again, do not judge the smells as good or bad, just observe them and notice they are there. You may notice individual smells such as the smell of food, your clothes, deodorant, perfume, or flowers or air fresheners that may be in the room. Or you might raise your hand or arm to notice the smell of your own skin. Explore all of these scents for a few moments and since the sense of smell is often one of the most neglected of the senses, it offers much in the cultivation of mindful awareness.

Taste: It is easy for your awareness to naturally flow from the sense of smell to that of taste as the two are so closely related and experienced. Perhaps, if you smelt food previously, you had already become aware of the sense of taste in an anticipatory way and had to guide your mind back from that to the smell itself. For now, become aware of the tastes in your mouth at this moment – perhaps you can taste your last drink or meal, or the lingering fresh taste of toothpaste or mouthwash. Observe the different tastes in different parts of your mouth – let your tongue explore your teeth and gums, the inside of your cheeks and lips. Explore mindfully for a few minutes.

N.B.: *You may wish to nibble on a small snack (for example a piece of fresh or dried fruit) or sip a drink for the taste part of the exercise.*

Sight: If you have not done so already, open your eyes and look at your environment afresh, with 'new born curiosity', perhaps as if it were the first time you have seen it all. Observe how light falls and reflects on different surfaces. Notice the different shapes, forms and textures – some simple, some complex, but do not analyse, just observe. Really notice the colours around you, perhaps the intensity and exact hue of some you have not noticed before in this way. You might reflect for a moment on any colours that may be missing. With your head kept still, finally just blink, widen your gaze and take in the whole visual scene for a minute as if appreciating a painting or a photograph in front of you.

Touch: Now guide your awareness to your hands. Where are they resting? What can you feel with your hands – the fabric of clothes, the armrests of your chair? Can you feel the warmth of the surface that your hands are touching, or is it cool? Perhaps feel a few surfaces or objects that are within reach, explore them through touch with non-judgemental 'new born curiosity'. It may help to close your eyes again at times to heighten the sense of touch and the ability to feel texture. Then become aware of the sensation of your body and the surfaces it is in contact with, as well as the feeling of the air surrounding your exposed skin.

Finally, guide your attention to the feeling of your feet, how they feel in your socks and shoes, and the sensation of weight or pressure as they make contact with the ground. In every sense at this moment you are 'grounded' in the moment. If you have not done so already, close your eyes and, with an awareness of your connection to both the ground and this moment, just breathe in a deep and relaxing manner for the final 2 minutes, enjoying the completion of this short journey of the senses.

This **'Complete Sensory Awareness'** meditation usually lasts around 15-25 minutes and is highly recommended for regular practice, especially when practised in different locations, or at any point where you wish to engage mindfully with the moment.

Many of my clients have found it a fantastic tool when they feel in life that they are on the metaphorical 'treadmill', and it is a way to simply step off for a moment and enjoy the stillness as you gather yourself mindfully.

Remember – Now take a moment to record your reflections on this morning's exercise in your workbook. Do not think too much about what to write, just write down your thoughts and feelings as they flow following the session.

If you can complete an evening session of this meditation exercise then I recommend doing so, but only if you have time.

Daily Practice

Daily Mantra: *"Relaxed mind, receptive mind"*

During today's everyday mindfulness, there is no one sensory theme, rather you are encouraged to experience your day mindfully with **all** the senses, in a state of 'open channel' receptivity to your environment, whatever may arise.

Embrace the day and look for new opportunities to enjoy moments of mindful awareness with all of your senses engaged. You may notice that some senses are stimulated more than others, and that is natural; but now you know to notice and explore what you might be overlooking.

These opportunities are often found in the everyday activities that we train our mind to complete on 'autopilot', often whilst we think about something else entirely.

There really is unlimited opportunity in even the most seemingly uneventful day. For example, a calming moment of morning mindfulness could come from an activity as simple as tying one's shoelaces.

Instead of simply rushing to tie them without even looking (perhaps whilst worrying about work or life), take advantage of the opportunity to connect with the moment that they offer. Stop for a moment, take a deep breath and focus on your shoes in front of you before you put them on. First look at your shoes, when did you last look at them in detail? Look at the sole, look inside. If a thought enters your mind that they look like they need repairing, acknowledge the thought, then let it go. You are not judging the shoes, but simply observing them. Perhaps feel their weight in your hands, the different textures on the surface. Maybe you can smell leather or polish. As you put them on slowly, feel the sensation of your foot entering each shoe. Feel for a moment how they feel without the laces tied. Then proceed to tie one set of laces. Look at the knot you are tying, notice the lace material, how it feels in your fingers. Now perhaps notice the feeling of your foot in the shoe, is it tighter, is there a pressure across your foot and where?

Before even moving on to the other shoe, this example shows how almost any everyday activity provides an opportunity to cultivate mindful awareness and bring us back into the present moment. Other simple opportunities for everyday mindfulness, including combining more than one sense, include:

- Brushing your teeth – taste, sound, touch, smell, even sight looking in the mirror.

- Making coffee or tea (watching the kettle boil, hearing the noise as it boils, watch when you pour, the tea/coffee infuses?)

- Focusing single-mindedly on tasks.

- Slow, mindful walking – breathing, smelling, listening and looking around as you walk.

- Mindful mealtimes and snacks.

- Awareness and gratitude for people around you…

Final Reflections: Your 7-Day Journey

As this is the final day of the *7-Day Mindfulness* programme, you should make time, perhaps in the evening, to reflect on the experience of the week as a whole.

In the final pages of the workbook you can record your personal reflections and summarise what you have learned, enjoyed and perhaps will build on in the future.

Continuing The Journey

Congratulations on completing the 7-Day Mindfulness programme!

For many, the week often becomes the starting point of a longer journey to explore the ongoing personal rewards and benefits of mindfulness.

These benefits can come from both incorporating more **everyday mindfulness** into your waking life, and setting aside time in your schedule for practising regular, dedicated **mindfulness meditation**. Likewise, mindfully adopting the **Key Attitudes** and the **Ideal State** of **'embracing the moment'** often has quite a profound and positive effect on an individual.

The exciting part of continuing your journey into mindfulness, and what it can do for you personally, is that there are so many different ways to explore it, both in terms of daily living and meditation.

For some, they achieve what they want from mindfulness by simply practising the 'Mindfulness of Breath' meditation exercise a few times a week. For others, they explore the many different mindfulness meditation techniques, perhaps starting a daily practice, or discover how mindfulness can help them overcome a problem or improve performance in an aspect of their life.

Learning More With Hypno-Mindfulness®

If you have enjoyed this approach to mindfulness you can explore other resources and further information available at:

http://www.hypno-mindfulness.com

The therapeutic benefits of mindfulness can also be experienced through private 1-2-1 sessions available at my clinic in Harley Street, London or group workshops for companies and organisations.

Since **Hypno-Mindfulness®** is highly influenced by my work as a Clinical Hypnotherapist, as well as guided meditation, I also incorporate teaching self-hypnosis to help make and sustain positive changes at the subconscious level.

Inspiring Others – Share Your Experience

As well as recommending *7-Day Mindfulness* to others who you think will benefit from it, you can also add your positive experiences during the week via the following link:

http://www.7daymindfulness.com/review.html

Reviews on Amazon are also much appreciated, plus you can share how you benefited from the programme on social media. The Twitter handle is **@7daymindfulness** and please use the hashtag **#7daymindfulness**.

Finally, thank you for exploring *7-Day Mindfulness* and I wish you well on your mindful journey.

Mindfulness: Scientific Studies

Bohlmeijer, E., Prenger, R., Taal, E., & Cuijpers, P. (2010). The effects of mindfulness-based stress reduction therapy on mental health of adults with a chronic medical disease: A meta-analysis. Journal of Psychosomatic Research, 68(6), 539-544.

Chiesa, A. & Serretti, A. (2011). Mindfulness based cognitive therapy for psychiatric disorders: A systematic review and meta-analysis. Psychiatry Research, 187(3), 441-453

Chiesa, A. & Serretti, A. (2009). Mindfulness-based stress reduction for stress management in healthy people: A review and meta-analysis. Journal of Alternative and Complementary Medicine, 15(5), 593-600.

Dekeyser, M., Raes, F., Leijssen, M., Leysen, S., & Dewulf, D. (2008). Mindfulness skills and interpersonal behaviour. Personality and Individual Differences, 44(5), 1235-1245.

Grossman, P., Niemann, L., Schmidt, S., & Walach, H. (2004). Mindfulness-based stress reduction and health benefits. A meta-analysis. Journal of Psychosomatic Research, 57(1), 35-43

Kluepfel, L., Ward, T., Yehuda, R., Dimoulas, E., Smith A., & Daly, K.(2013) The evaluation of mindfulness-based stress reduction for veterans with mental health conditions. Journal of Holistic Nursing. [Epub ahead of print].

Ledesma, D. & Kumano, H. (2009). Mindfulness-based stress reduction and cancer: A meta-analysis. Psycho-oncology, 18(6), 571-579.

Marchand, W. R. (2012). Mindfulness-based stress reduction, mindfulness-based cognitive therapy, and zen meditation for depression, anxiety, pain, and psychological distress. Journal of Psychiatric Practice, 18(4), 233-252.

Vago, D.R. & Nakamura, Y. (2011). Selective attentional bias towards pain-related threat in fibromyalgia: preliminary evidence for effects of mindfulness meditation training. Cognitive Therapy Research, 35(6), 581-594.

Winbush, N. Y., Gross, C. R., & Kreitzer, M. J. (2007). The effects of mindfulness-based stress reduction on sleep disturbance: A systematic review. Explore, 3(6), 585-591.

Zgierska, A., Rabago, D., Chawla, N., Kushner, K., Koehler, R., & Marlatt, A. (2009). Mindfulness meditation for substance use disorders: A systematic review. Substance Abuse, 30(4), 266-294.

HYPNO·MINDFULNESS®

7-Day

Mindfulness

Workbook

7-Day Mindfulness: **Key Attitudes**

During the next 7 days, I will be mindful to adopt and incorporate the attitudes below in the following ways.

Patience

_____
_____
_____
_____
_____
_____
_____

Trust

_____
_____
_____
_____
_____
_____

Non-Judgment

_____
_____
_____
_____
_____
_____
_____

Acceptance

_____
_____
_____
_____
_____
_____
_____

Non-Attachment

_____
_____
_____
_____
_____
_____
_____

'New Born' Curiosity

_____
_____
_____
_____
_____
_____
_____

I will acknowledge my thoughts and feelings, embracing the moment and trust in my ability to simply let... them... go.

Signed _____ **Date** _____

Day 1: Awakening Awareness

HYPNO-MINDFULNESS®

✓ Patience ✓ Trust ✓ Non-Judgment ✓ Acceptance

✓ Non-Attachment ✓ 'New Born' Curiosity ✓ *Embracing The Moment*

Morning Meditation – Reflections   Time spent: _____

How I Felt Before

_____
_____
_____
_____

How I Felt After

_____
_____
_____
_____

My Thoughts & Feelings

_____
_____
_____
_____

Daily Practice – Reflections

_____
_____
_____
_____
_____
_____

Additional Notes

_____

_____

_____

_____

_____

_____

_____

_____

_____

_____

_____

_____

_____

_____

_____

_____

_____

How I Will Apply What I Have Learned

_____

_____

_____

_____

_____

_____

_____

_____

Day 2: Mindfulness of Sight

✓ Patience ✓ Trust ✓ Non-Judgment ✓ Acceptance

✓ Non-Attachment ✓ 'New Born' Curiosity ✓ *Embracing The Moment*

Morning Meditation – Reflections   Time spent: _____

How I Felt Before

_____
_____
_____
_____

How I Felt After

_____
_____
_____
_____

My Thoughts & Feelings

_____
_____
_____
_____

Daily Practice – Reflections

_____
_____
_____
_____
_____
_____

Additional Notes

_____

_____

_____

_____

_____

_____

_____

_____

_____

_____

_____

_____

_____

_____

_____

_____

_____

How I Will Apply What I Have Learned

_____

_____

_____

_____

_____

_____

_____

_____

Day 3: Mindfulness of Sound

✓ Patience ✓ Trust ✓ Non-Judgment ✓ Acceptance

✓ Non-Attachment ✓ 'New Born' Curiosity ✓ *Embracing The Moment*

Morning Meditation – Reflections   Time spent: _____

How I Felt Before

_____

_____

_____

_____

How I Felt After

_____

_____

_____

_____

My Thoughts & Feelings

_____

_____

_____

_____

Daily Practice – Reflections

_____

_____

_____

_____

_____

_____

Additional Notes

_____
_____
_____
_____
_____
_____
_____
_____
_____
_____
_____
_____
_____
_____
_____
_____
_____

How I Will Apply What I Have Learned

_____
_____
_____
_____
_____
_____
_____
_____

Day 4: Mindfulness of Taste

✓ Patience ✓ Trust ✓ Non-Judgment ✓ Acceptance

✓ Non-Attachment ✓ 'New Born' Curiosity ✓ *Embracing The Moment*

Morning Meditation – Reflections   Time spent: _____

How I Felt Before

_____

_____

_____

_____

How I Felt After

_____

_____

_____

_____

My Thoughts & Feelings

_____

_____

_____

_____

Daily Practice – Reflections

_____

_____

_____

_____

_____

_____

Additional Notes

_____

_____

_____

_____

_____

_____

_____

_____

_____

_____

_____

_____

_____

_____

_____

_____

_____

How I Will Apply What I Have Learned

_____

_____

_____

_____

_____

_____

_____

_____

Day 5: **Mindfulness of Touch**

✓ Patience ✓ Trust ✓ Non-Judgment ✓ Acceptance

✓ Non-Attachment ✓ 'New Born' Curiosity ✓ *Embracing The Moment*

Morning Meditation – Reflections   Time spent: _____

How I Felt Before

_____

_____

_____

_____

How I Felt After

_____

_____

_____

_____

My Thoughts & Feelings

_____

_____

_____

_____

Daily Practice – Reflections

_____

_____

_____

_____

_____

_____

Additional Notes

_____
_____
_____
_____
_____
_____
_____
_____
_____
_____
_____
_____
_____
_____
_____
_____
_____
_____

How I Will Apply What I Have Learned

_____
_____
_____
_____
_____
_____
_____
_____
_____

Day 6: Mindfulness of Smell

✓ Patience ✓ Trust ✓ Non-Judgment ✓ Acceptance

✓ Non-Attachment ✓ 'New Born' Curiosity ✓ *Embracing The Moment*

Morning Meditation – Reflections   Time spent: _____

How I Felt Before

_____
_____
_____
_____

How I Felt After

_____
_____
_____
_____

My Thoughts & Feelings

_____
_____
_____
_____

Daily Practice – Reflections

_____
_____
_____
_____
_____
_____

Additional Notes

_____
_____
_____
_____
_____
_____
_____
_____
_____
_____
_____
_____
_____
_____
_____
_____

How I Will Apply What I Have Learned

_____
_____
_____
_____
_____
_____
_____
_____
_____

Day 7: Receptive Reflection

HYPNO-MINDFULNESS®

✓ Patience ✓ Trust ✓ Non-Judgment ✓ Acceptance

✓ Non-Attachment ✓ 'New Born' Curiosity ✓ *Embracing The Moment*

Morning Meditation – Reflections   Time spent: _____

How I Felt Before

_____

_____

_____

_____

How I Felt After

_____

_____

_____

_____

My Thoughts & Feelings

_____

_____

_____

_____

Daily Practice – Reflections

_____

_____

_____

_____

_____

_____

Additional Notes

_____
_____
_____
_____
_____
_____
_____
_____
_____
_____
_____
_____
_____
_____
_____
_____
_____
_____

How I Will Apply What I Have Learned

_____
_____
_____
_____
_____
_____
_____
_____

Final Reflections: Your 7-Day Journey

Having completed this short but powerful exploration of mindfulness and sensory awareness, it is common to experience many new or re-invigorated thoughts, feelings and ideas.

For some it is a renewed sense of calm, clarity or a different perspective on their life and the world around them. For others, it is a discovering or re-discovering of their 'body-mind' connection or simply feeling more in touch with themselves.

However, just as each person is unique, each **7-Day Mindfulness** journey is unique, so it can be useful to write below a short summary of the whole experience for you personally. You might include what you have learned, what you especially enjoyed, and what you may continue to do on an ongoing basis to cultivate mindful awareness.

7-Day Mindfulness: *My Personal Reflections*

_____

_____

_____

_____

_____

_____

_____

_____

_____

_____

_____

_____

_____

_____

_____

_____

_____

Inspire: **Share Your Experience**

HYPNO-MINDFULNESS®

If you have enjoyed **7-Day Mindfulness** there are a couple of ways you can inspire others to take their own beneficial journey into mindfulness using the programme.

It is always exciting to share and hear about different people's experiences, both of mindfulness meditation and especially opportunities for everyday mindfulness.

As well as reviewing the book online via Amazon, you can also submit your own thoughts and experiences at:

http://www.7daymindfulness.com/review.html

Lastly, you can inspire others on social media with a short tweet on Twitter about the benefits you experienced from embracing your senses and mindfulness in this way.

Within the 140 character limit you could simply finish the sentence, **"I discovered…"** or **"I learned…"**, explaining how you benefited personally from the **7-Day Mindfulness** programme. If possible, try and use the **#7daymindfulness** hashtag.

Twitter

@7daymindfulness

#7daymindfulness

Thank you and for further information on my approach please visit:

www.hypno-mindfulness.com

#0109 - 111016 - C0 - 210/148/5 - PB - DID1611655